HAWKS and FALCONS

Karen Haywood

Marshall Cavendish
Benchmark

New York

Marshall Cavendish Benchmark
99 White Plains Road
Tarrytown, New York 10591
www.marshallcavendish.us

All websites were available and accurate when this book was sent to press.

Publisher: Michelle Bisson
Art Director: Anahid Hamparian
Series Design by: Elynn Cohen
Cover Design: Kay Petronio

Library of Congress Cataloging-in-Publication Data

Haywood, Karen.
Hawks and falcons / by Karen Haywood.
p. cm. -- (Endangered!)
Includes bibliographical references and index.
Summary: "Describes the characteristics, behaviors, and plights of hawks and falcons, and what people can do to help"--Provided
by publisher.
ISBN 978-0-7614-4051-2
1.   Hawks--Juvenile literature. 2. Falcons--Juvenile literature. I. Title.
QL696.F32H394 2011
598.9'44--dc22
2009020340

Front cover: Goshawk
Back cover: Prairie Falcon (top), Osprey (bottom)

Photo research by Paulee Kestin
Front cover: Getty Images
The photographs in this book are used by permission and through the courtesy of: Alamy: Scott Buckel, 1; Stock Connection
Blue, 14; Natural Visions, 16; Arco Images GmbH, 18; BristolK, 19; joel zatz, 20; blickwinkel/McPHOTO/MAS, 26; Danita
Delimont, 28; Juniors Bildarchiv, 36; imagebroker, 40. Getty: Joseph Van Os, back cover (top); Gail Shumway, back cover (bot-
tom); Arthur Morris, 8; AFP, 42. Photo Researchers: Jim Zipp, 9, 12. Corbis: Eric Hosking, 10; Galen Rowell, 33. Lloyd Spitalnik: 6.
Vireo: R. & N. Bowers, 22; B Gozansky, 34; A. Morris, 37; A. & J. Binns, 45.
Printed in Malaysia (T)
1 2 3 4 5 6

Contents

Introduction

Hawks and falcons are among the most awe-inspiring birds in the world. Watching them soar and dive through the skies is a wonderful sight. Hawks and falcons, like eagles, are considered raptors, or birds of **prey**. The word "raptor" is from the Latin *rapere*, which means "to seize."

All hawks and falcons have certain basic similarities. Raptors are carnivorous, which means they eat only meat. In order to survive, they must hunt and capture their prey. To aid them in doing so, hawks and falcons have very good eyesight and can see their prey from a great distance away. Hawks and falcons have strong **talons**—or claws—used to grab the prey and hold on tight. The birds' sharp, hooked beaks are perfect for tearing apart the food and eating it.

We know a lot about birds today because of the science called ornithology. Ornithologists study birds from all angles. They study how birds live in their environment, birds' bodies, and how they interact with each other. Topics also researched include changes in populations of birds across continents, how birds changed over the centuries and what their ancestors looked like, the ways birds are changing in today's environment, and how they may be affected by changes in the environment today.

Birds have lived on, and flown above, this planet for millions of years. During that time, the Earth has experienced several environmental changes. Many scientists today feel that the latest environmental changes have been caused by human behavior. We have been burning too much coal, gas, and oil, and we continue to clear forests that are the homes to hawks, falcons, bears, eagles, and other **endangered** animals.

Over the past five hundred years, close to five hundred bird **species,** or types, have not been able to adapt to the changes in their environment. As a result, these species have become **extinct.** That is an average of one bird species disappearing each year. During this century, scientists predict that ten species of birds will disappear each year. There are about 290 species of falcons and hawks in the world today. Many are in danger of disappearing forever.

1

Cooper's Hawks

The Cooper's Hawk is a medium-sized forest hawk. This type of hawk can be found in most of the United States, northern Mexico, and southern Canada. It is called a forest hawk because it lives in the trees. It has a long tail and short, rounded wings so that it can fly quickly around the tree trunks and between the branches.

Female Cooper's Hawks measure about 16 to 19 inches (41 to 47 centimeters) long and weigh up to 24 ounces (680 grams). The females are a little larger than the males. Males measure between 14 and 16 inches (37 and 41 cm) and weigh between 10 and 14 ounces (302

Cooper's Hawks have distinctive coloring in their feathers and on their legs.

and 402 g). The **wingspan** of the Cooper's Hawk averages around 28 to 35 inches (70 to 90 cm).

The head of this hawk is mostly black or dark gray, but the tips of the feathers are a light brown or cinnamon color. The chest is usually red in color. The rest of the bird, when in flight, appears to be striped, with a wide, white band on the tip of the tail. The most interesting physical characteristic of the Cooper's Hawk is the color of its eyes. When the hawks are very young their eyes are yellow or light orange. As the bird grows older the eyes darken, becoming orange or red.

These hawks live in the trees, but prefer to be on the edge of a

Young Cooper's Hawks have light yellow eyes.

Feather patterns make the bird's wings look striped.

large, dense forest. They build their broad, flat nests of sticks in trees near clearings, roads, lakes, or streams. From their hidden perch up in the trees, they use their keen eyesight to spot their food. The diet of Cooper's Hawks consists mostly of smaller birds, but in some areas it may include small animals and lizards.

IN DANGER

The Cooper's Hawk population, like that of many eagles and other birds of prey, declined due to environmental pollution in the 1950s and 1960s. This pollution included chemicals, such as DDT, which were used to kill insects and other pests. These harmful chemicals caused the

Sharp talons help the hawk catch food. These hawks were sometimes called chicken hawks because farmers thought they used their talons to hunt chickens.

hawks' eggshells to become thin and break easily. This means that healthy chicks were not able to hatch, and the population could not increase. In addition to the poisoning by **pesticides** and pollution, this hawk, which is also called the chicken hawk, was shot by farmers who accused them of stealing their chickens.

By the late 1960s, many believed that Cooper's Hawks were close to extinction. Since then, legal protection for the birds has improved the hawks' future. Although the Cooper's Hawk is listed as extirpated (wiped out), endangered, or of special concern in twelve states in the United States, recent studies report they are on their way to recovery. One reason may be because some are moving from the forests, which are being destroyed for roads and shopping malls. Many experts think that Cooper's Hawks are building nests closer to cities and are learning to adapt to the new environment.

2

Northern Goshawks

The Northern Goshawk's natural habitat is the northern and western regions of North America, parts of northern Europe and Asia, and on some of the mountains of Mexico and Iran. This bird is a very powerful raptor and is the largest of all North American hawks.

The Goshawk has broad wings and a long tail. Its coloring includes various shades of gray and white. Its chin, throat, and chest are a pale gray and the tail is dark gray above and pale below. It appears to be striped when in flight. Females measure 21 to 24 inches (53 to 62 cm) long and weigh up to 43 ounces (1.2 kg). Males measure between 18 and 20 inches (46 and 51 cm) long and weigh

Northern Goshawks in North America are the largest of all the hawks in the region, and are fierce predators.

Goshawks hatch and raise their chicks—or babies—in nests high up in the trees.

between 24 and 36 ounces (677 and 1,014 g). The wingspan of the Northern Goshawk averages around 38 to 45 inches (98 to 115 cm). Its eyes are orange-red when young, and like the eyes of the Cooper's Hawk, turn dark red when it is older.

Since the range of the Goshawk is so large and covers so much of the world, its preferred habitat varies quite a bit. For the most part, however, this hawk chooses tall trees for nesting. The trees may be oak, spruce, pine, or aspen, as long as they provide small, open areas for hunting. If possible, this hawk will use the same nest year after year.

The diet of the Goshawk is also varied. This hawk will dine on other birds—especially grouse, jays, crows, and thrushes—and small animals, such as squirrels and rabbits. When no birds or mammals are available, the hawks will eat reptiles and insects. But whatever they choose to hunt, they do it in one of two ways. They either perch and watch from a high vantage point and then quickly attack, or they chase down their prey. These hawks fly with exceptional speed until they catch their prey.

The Northern Goshawk has not suffered from pesticide pollution as have other birds. However, it has lost its habitat in the Pacific Northwest of the United States and other places because of forest destruction. Many forests are cut down and cleared so that the trees can be used for lumber and to make space for roads, houses, or business areas. People interested in protecting the hawks have helped to increase the public's awareness of the hawks' small populations. In some places, Northern Goshawk nests are kept secret so that the hawks can be protected from humans who might hurt them.

3

Ospreys

Unlike other hawks that have three toes on each foot, the Osprey has four powerful toes of about equal length. The fourth toe is opposable, which means it can move around so that it is opposite from another toe. This helps the bird to grasp and hold objects more easily. All of the Osprey's toes have needle-sharp black claws. The soles of the gray feet are covered with short, spinelike scales that help this fish hawk grasp and carry slippery fish.

Ospreys are mostly brown on their backs and have white chests. This hawk has a white head with a bold black stripe around the eyes that continues down the sides of the

Ospreys are great hunters both on land and in the water.

Ospreys can have very large wingspans.

head. Female Ospreys usually have dark spotted feathers around their necks that look a little like a necklace. Ospreys measure 20 to 25 inches (51 to 62 cm) long and weigh up to 4.2 pounds (1.9 kg). Although the female is larger than the male, the size difference is fairly small. The wingspan of the Osprey is a little over 5 feet (1.5 meters). When in flight, the long, narrow wings of the Osprey form an "M" shape.

Since Ospreys depend on fish for their food, they are usually found near water—along the coasts of oceans, lakes,

In the wild, Ospreys will build their nests in tall trees overlooking water.

marshes, and rivers. The water must be clear and the fish must swim close to the surface so that the Osprey can capture them. Ospreys prefer to build their nests in dead or open-topped live trees that are very near, or even in, the water. But if such trees are not available, Ospreys will choose rocky outcrops, cliffs, or even human-made structures like utility poles, channel markers, or special platforms built just for them. For example, two-thirds of the Ospreys in

Some people put platforms at the top of utility poles to give Ospreys a place to nest.

Wisconsin nest on structures built by humans who want to encourage the birds to nest and reproduce.

The Osprey population is relatively healthy now, but it was a different story just a few years ago. The use of the insecticide DDT after World War II caused Osprey eggshells to become thin and easily broken. This meant that few chicks survived to become healthy adults. DDT is no longer used in the United States. However, problems for the Ospreys today include habitat destruction along the coasts, and water pollution that kills the fish they eat. Ospreys are still listed as a species of "special concern" in several places. Though they are not endangered, their populations are still in danger of becoming very small.

4

Kites

As its name suggests, the range of the Mississippi Kite includes the Mississippi River valley in the United States. This graceful, medium-sized hawk also lives and breeds in parts of the southwestern and southeastern United States. Mississippi Kites can also be found in some parts of eastern Mexico and Central America. In search of warmer weather during the winter, many Mississippi Kites migrate to South America, sometimes as far south as northern Argentina.

The main physical difference between kites and other hawks is that kites do not have the bony ridge that

The Mississippi Kite is one of several endangered animal species that live along the Mississippi Valley.

is found over the eye of most other hawks. Kites' feet are adapted for taking small prey like insects, which they catch while soaring through the air. In fact, the Mississippi Kite has been called the "insect specialist" because of its talent for catching and eating insects, such as grasshoppers and dragonflies while in flight. This bird will also catch and eat bats, toads, lizards, and frogs. But for the most part, Mississippi Kites prefer insects.

The Mississippi Kite has a light-colored, sometimes white, head and chest. Its back and long, narrow wings are gray, and it has black, forked tail feathers. Males and females are similar in size, measuring 12 to 15 inches (31 to 37 cm) long. They may weigh up to 13 ounces (372 g). The wingspan of the Mississippi Kite averages around 29 to 33 inches (75 to 83 cm). Its eyes are deep red with a dark spot in front of them that makes the eyes appear very large.

The populations of Mississippi Kites were on the decline in the mid-1900s, partly due to people who enjoyed the hobby of egg collecting. Since the kite's nest could be easily reached in some places, many egg collectors took them, even though the birds and their eggs were protected by certain laws and state regulations. The kites' populations were hit hard, and to this day, they are still listed as **threatened** or endangered in some states. Many experts hope to increase kite populations by protecting the birds' nests and natural habitats. Laws that have been passed make sure that only people with special permits—usually scientists and **conservationists**—can do anything to interefere with the kites' nests.

SNAIL KITE

The snail kite, also called the Everglade Kite, is a medium-sized hawk that lives part of the year in Florida. It prefers the freshwater marshes of southern Florida around Lake Okeechobee. This kite also lives in Cuba, Mexico, and parts of South America. As its name suggests, this hawk has a very specialized diet—freshwater apple snails. The snail kite hovers above the water until it spies a snail on the stem of a marsh plant. The kite then extends its talons and grasps the snail from the plant. It then flies away to a

Snail kites get their name from the type of food they eat. Their sharp beaks help them get to the meat of the snail inside the shell.

high perch where it twists the shell away from the snail and uses its sharply curved beak to eat its prey. If apple snails are not available, the snail kite will also eat freshwater crabs, turtles, and small rodents.

The male and female snail kites look quite different from one another. The male is dark gray with a black head. The tips of its wings are black and it has bright red legs and eyes. The female is a brownish-gray color with some white markings on its head. It legs and eyes are bright orange. Both male and female snail kites have very striking white bands on their tails that are visible when the birds are in flight. Males and females are similar in size, measuring 16 to 19 inches (41 to 47 cm) long and weighing between 12 and 21 ounces (340 and 520 g). The wingspan of the snail kite averages around 41 to 44 inches (104 to 112 cm).

Snail kites build very loosely constructed nests of sticks, which may be built on the ground, in shrubbery, or in a tree. Wherever they build their nest, it must be close to water that has apple snails. In the past, there was plenty of freshwater marsh in Florida and therefore, many apple snails to feed this hawk. In the 1900s, however, the destruction and drainage of more than a million acres of these marshes decreased the snail population. With their food source depleted, the snail kites also suffered. Because of the loss of habitat and food, the snail kite was placed on the Endangered Species list in March 1967. Conservationists and scientists are trying to protect the kites' habitat and natural prey, but the populations still remain small. However, some kite populations can still be found around the Everglades and in some wildlife refuges in Florida.

5

Aplomado and Prairie Falcons

The Aplomado Falcon is a medium-sized bird that lives in the open plains, grasslands, and savannas. By the 1940s, populations of this falcon were wiped out in the United States. Scientists believe that loss of habitat led to the falcons' disappearance.

The Aplomado Falcon is a multicolored bird with a dark gray back and upper wings. *Aplomado* is Spanish for "lead-colored" or "dark gray," which is how the bird got its

Most Aplomado Falcons will not build their own nests. Instead, they will live in the abandoned nests of ravens, hawks, and kites.

name. Above each eye, the falcon has a white dash that extends to the back of its head. This bird has a long black tail—much longer than the tails of most falcons—and a white upper body with a black band across the middle. To many, this black band resembles a wide belt. The Aplomado Falcon has cinnamon-orange-colored markings on its head and belly. A yellow ring surrounds the eyes, which can be brown, hazel, or a dark yellowish brown. Young Aplomado Falcons have a blue ring around their eyes.

Males and females are similar in size, measuring 14 to 18 inches (35 to 45 cm) long. Adult falcons can weigh between 8.4 and 16 ounces (208 and 460 g). The wingspan of the Aplomado Falcon averages about 31 to 40 inches (78 to 102 cm). This falcon is similar in size to the American crow.

Aplomado Falcons prefer a diet of birds, insects, and the occasional bat. They will also steal food from other hawks and falcons. Mated pairs of Aplomado Falcons will hunt together as a team. Food that is not eaten will be hidden for later meals.

Aplomados were once common in the American Southwest, from southern Texas to eastern Arizona, but by the middle of the twentieth century they had disappeared. There was hope that many would survive in the Chihuahuan Desert of Mexico, but because of recent droughts and destruction of their breeding grounds by farmers, scientists fear that the falcons will soon disappear from Mexico. Farming in the Tarabillas Valley of Mexico has destroyed at least seven of these falcons' breeding regions.

The Aplomado Falcon was declared an endangered species in the United States in 1985. In 1993, a private conservation fund began releasing Aplomado Falcons into southern Texas. These falcons had been born and bred in captivity. As a result of these conservation efforts, there are currently more than forty established nesting pairs in the region. Two distinct areas of population now exist. One is centered in the Laguna Atascosa Wildlife Area near Brownsville, and the other is on Matagorda Island near Rockport. It will be several years before scientists know just how successful these efforts to save the Aplomado Falcon have been.

PRAIRIE FALCONS

The Prairie Falcon is native to North America. This large falcon's range covers most of the western United States, parts of western Canada, and about half of central Mexico. The desert foothills and mountains are the Prairie Falcon's habitat. The falcons reuse the nest they used the year before or, if they are young, they may use the abandoned nest of a raven. These nests are almost always found on cliffs or bluffs.

These falcons are about 14 to 20 inches (37 to 51 cm) long, with the females growing a little larger than the males. Adults weigh between 1 and 3 pounds (510 g and 1 kg). The wingspan of the Prairie Falcon reaches 35 to 44 inches (90 to 113 cm). This bird is mostly pale brown in color, with a whitish chest with brown spots and bars. It has dark patches of feathers in several places—above the beak, on the sides of its head, and under each wing. Its eyes are dark brown surrounded by yellow rings.

For food, this falcon prefers small mammals and small- to medium-sized birds. The mammals include ground squirrels, pocket gophers, and baby rabbits and

Prairie falcons often make or use nests tucked away in holes or cracks in cliffs and bluffs.

hares. The birds they eat include species of lark, quail, mourning doves, burrowing owls, and swifts. In some desert areas, lizards, snakes, and even tortoises may be eaten.

But Prairie Falcons themselves are the prey of humans. Unfortunately, poachers and hunters shoot them for sport, even though it is illegal. Also, some populations are harmed by the side effects of mining, farming, and development that destroy their habitat and food supply. Many local conservation groups are working to save the Prairie Falcon and its habitat.

Gyrfalcons

The Gyrfalcon (pronounced *jerfalcon)* is the largest true falcon in the world. It ranges from 19 to 24 inches (50 to 61 cm) in length and weighs between 2.2 and 4.6 pounds (1 and 2 kg). The wingspan of a Gyrfalcon may reach 51 inches (130 cm), which is more than 4 feet! This bird has a variety of feather colors: white, black, blackish-brown, or gray, with gray being the most common. Its coloring, however, is not what distinguishes it from other falcons. Its very large size and the fact that its head is pale without the "hooded" look of other falcons makes it

Not only is it the largest true falcon, but the Gyrfalcon also has distinctive pale coloring.

Gyrfalcons' sharp eyesight help them spot prey from the sky.

easier to identify. The Gyrfalcon has dark brown eyes surrounded by yellow rings, and yellow or orange legs.

This species lives in lands far to the north, in the arctic and subarctic tundra and taiga regions of North America, Greenland, Iceland, and northern Europe and Asia—all around the northern parts of the world. They are accustomed to the extreme cold. Some may even nest and lay eggs when the temperature is below 0 degrees Fahrenheit (-17.7 degrees Celsius), and they sometimes bathe in the runoff water of frozen rivers. That is a seriously chilly birdbath!

In colder regions with fewer trees, Gyrfalcons often nest along rocky cliffs and outcroppings.

Rarely does the Gyrfalcon build a nest of its own, but will use the abandoned nest of a raven, buzzard, or golden eagle. In far north regions where there are few or no trees, the Gyrfalcon will lay and shelter its eggs in a depression on cliff ledges or on human-made structures, such as oil pipelines.

The Gyrfalcon prefers other birds for its food, from tiny finches, passerines, and seagulls to large geese, cranes, and auks. Its favorite bird is the ptarmigan, a kind of grouse. This falcon also eats small mammals like arctic hares, lemmings, and ground squirrels. It uses four different ways to hunt its prey: flying low for a surprise attack; chasing prey for a long time over a long distance, which tires out the prey so that it gives up from exhaustion; hovering and making short stoops to force prey from its hiding place; or shooting up from below into the middle of a flock of birds. When chasing other birds, it will knock them to the ground rather than grabbing them in midair.

The Gyrfalcon has been a popular bird for the sport of falconry for centuries. (Falconry is a sport that uses trained falcons to hunt smaller animals.) Genghis Khan, a thirteenth-century warlord, often carried a white Gyrfalcon. England's King Richard I took his falcons with him on the Crusades. It is said that after he was captured by the enemy, part of his ransom was two white Gyrfalcons.

Today, the falconry market for this bird poses a threat to its survival in Scandinavia, Canada, and Russia. Poachers illegally capture these birds to sell to falconers, which reduces the Gyrfalcon populations in the wild. Many conservation groups are working to put a stop to this practice by appealing to the governments of the countries where this practice occurs.

7

Peregrine Falcons

From great heights, this falcon can dive at speeds approaching 250 miles per hour (402 kilometers per hour) to capture its prey. A medium-sized bird, the Peregrine weighs between 1 and 2.1 pounds (453 and 952 g) and measures between 14 and 18 inches (37 and 46 cm) long, with a 37 to 46 inch (94 to 116 cm) wingspan. As with some other species of hawks and falcons, the female is larger than the male.

Peregrines can be found in many places worldwide since they breed almost everywhere. Their numbers, however, are still low in many places.

Peregrines are natural hunters, but injured or orphaned birds sometimes need to be trained to hunt before being released back into the wild.

Since the Peregrine lives on all continents, except Antarctica, there are some differences in feather coloring throughout the different ranges. All adult Peregrines, however, have dark heads that make them look as though they are wearing a hood. Their back feathers are a bluish gray, and their chests are white with dark stripes, or bars. They have dark brown eyes with yellow eye rings and yellow legs.

Peregrine Falcons mostly eat birds, the type of which vary according to location. Since the Peregrine can carry prey that weighs almost as much as it does itself, some prey are rather large, such as ducks, auks, seagulls, parrots, crows, pigeons, and doves. This falcon is famous for how it hunts. Almost all prey is killed in midflight after the falcon selects its target and dives at speeds of 200 miles per hour (322 km per hour) or more.

The favored nesting sites of the Peregrine Falcon are usually high, rocky cliff ledges in out-of-the-way places overlooking a lake, stream, or river. There, they will scrape a bowl-like nest in the rock. They may also nest on the rooftops or ledges of city buildings or in the steelwork of bridges. They have been observed hunting at night around the Empire State Building in New York City.

The word *peregrine* means "wanderer" or "traveler," and this falcon lives up to its name. It may migrate, or move, 15,500 miles (25,000 km) in one year. In fact, one source notes that it is easier to list where they are not, than where they are. Unfortunately, because of the use of DDT in the 1940s, 1950s, and 1960s, the Peregrine was virtually eliminated throughout much of North America, especially east of the Rocky Mountains and south of the

Canadian Arctic. In 1970, the Peregrine Falcon was added to the Endangered Species list in the United States.

The same year, in order to prevent the extinction of this amazing bird, Tom Cade, an ornithologist at Cornell University, developed methods to breed falcons in captivity. The Peregrine Fund was established by the university from donations received from generous people who were also hoping to prevent the disappearance of these falcons.

Over the next thirty years, many people and organizations worked hard to reintroduce the Peregrine to its natural habitat. Thanks to rules of the Endangered Species Act, the 1972 act that outlawed the use of DDT, and a recovery program that involved federal and state wildlife agencies, universities, conservation organizations, and falconry clubs, thousands of chicks were bred and raised in captivity. When they were old enough, they were released into the wild. This effort was so successful that in 1999, with more than 1,600 nesting pairs nationwide, the U.S. Fish and Wildlife Service removed the Peregrine Falcon from the federal Endangered Species List. The

Peregrine falcons have been known to nest on buildings and other structures in big cities.

birds are still protected by local laws in Illinois, Indiana, New Jersey, Wisconsin, and a number of other states where population goals have not been met. These positive results—from people working together to save the Peregrines—show that there may still be hope for other endangered hawks and falcons.

GLOSSARY

conservationist—A person who preserves or protects something, such as an animal or habitat.

endangered—Any species that is in danger of extinction throughout all or a significant portion of its range.

extinct—No longer existing.

pesticide—A substance used to destroy pests, such as insects or other small animals.

prey—Animals that are hunted and used as food.

species—A specific type of animal. For example, a Gyrfalcon is a species of falcon.

talon—The claw of an animal—especially of a bird of prey.

threatened—In the case of animals, to be at risk of becoming endangered.

wingspan—The distance from the tip of one wing to the tip of the other wing.

FIND OUT MORE

Books

Evert, Laura, and Wayne Lynch. *Birds of Prey: Explore the Fascinating Worlds of Eagles, Falcons, Owls, and Vultures.* Minnetonka, MN: NorthWord, 2005.

Gunzi, Christiane. *The Best Book of Endangered and Extinct Animals.* New York: Kingfisher, 2004.

Hickman, Pamela. *Birds of Prey Rescue: Changing the Future for Endangered Wildlife.* Richmond Hill, Ontario: Firefly Books, 2006.

Websites

Carolina Raptor Center
http://www.carolinaraptorcenter.org

Hawk Mountain Sanctuary
http://www.hawkmountain.org

Kids' Planet—Defenders of Wildlife
http://www.kidsplanet.org

The Peregrine Fund
http://www.peregrinefund.org

INDEX

Page numbers in **boldface** are illustrations.

ABOUT THE AUTHOR

Karen Haywood has edited and written many books for young readers. She lives in North Carolina where she watches the squirrels steal fruit from the apple trees in her backyard as she writes. Inspired by the first Earth Day in 1970, she has been a strong advocate for the environment and animal rights for many years.